Barbara Drake G 413

Welcome to
BEDPAN ALLEY

Copyright © by PANACHE PRODUCTIONS and EAGLE FEATURES
All rights reserved.
PANACHE PRODUCTIONS 1388 Moorpark Road, Thousand Oaks, California 91360
Printed in Canada: 1984

Frank Ridgeway and Frank Heron
WELCOME TO BEDPAN ALLEY

ISBN 0-7701-0298-0

Published in Canada by Paperjacks Limited

Welcome to BEDPAN ALLEY

By Frank Ridgeway and Frank Heron

PaperJacks LTD.
Markham, Ontario, Canada

WELCOME TO BEDPAN ALLEY is respectfully dedicated to Doctors in Doctor Places everywhere.

It is also dedicated to Nurses, registered, un-registered and even the home variety usually played by Mothers, but in this day of equality, sometimes by Fathers.

But mainly, we dedicate our book to those who are ill, and to those hypochondriacs who THINK they are ill. They too, suffer.

We hope the book will bring you a bit of laughter, that you might suffer a bit less.

Last, but most important, we ask you to recall the old proposition:

"HE WHO LAUGHS.........LASTS"

This cartoon of Frank Ridgeway is modelled after the real life cartoonist, Frank Ridgeway.

For more than 25 years he has created the King Features syndicated cartoon strip Mr. Abernathy

Mr. Ridgeway brings, as his personal pain contributions, a heart attack (in Bermuda on a golfing trip), an appendix removal, and a fistula operation which is now behind him.

Humor helped him through each time.

In fact, as a comedy cartoonist, it paid the bills.

This cartoon character of Frank Heron is based on the real life Frank Heron, who has written and directed comedy programs with Jonathan Winters, Lilly Tomlin, Harvey Korman, Rich Little and hundreds of others too funny to mention.

Or not funny enough!

He brings, as his personal pain contributions, one broken neck, TWO hernia operations, and a circumcision late enough in life to be too painful to regard as anything other than funny.

The two creators of this book suffer at still another level. They are both golfers.

This idea for a book on pain, suffering, and the indignities of the hospital routine, doesn't sound as though it would hold much promise for laughter.

Our book does not laugh AT these terrible things.

It has been designed with one simple thought...to let you know that you don't suffer alone.

Somewhere (in every hospital) an orderly is about to begin that gross event known as "shaving-for-the-operation."

Somewhere, a trainee is jabbing the OTHER arm, looking for a vein, in vain. And yes, somewhere, you can be sure, a nurse will wake a patient from a deep sleep to offer a sleeping pill.

We've been patients.

We've been involved with every phase of hospital routine pictured in this book.

Welllllll....almost.

Frank just reminded me (never mind which Frank, it's always the other one) that there are SOME situations we only know from hear-say.

Neither of us has ever been pregnant.

We wish you laughter.

It helps to heal.

Welcome to...

BEDPAN ALLEY

At last.
We're in. And settled.

The hospital routine is about to start, so first, let's meet our nurses.

"THANK YOU, NURSE, FOR FLUFFING UP MY PILLOW!"

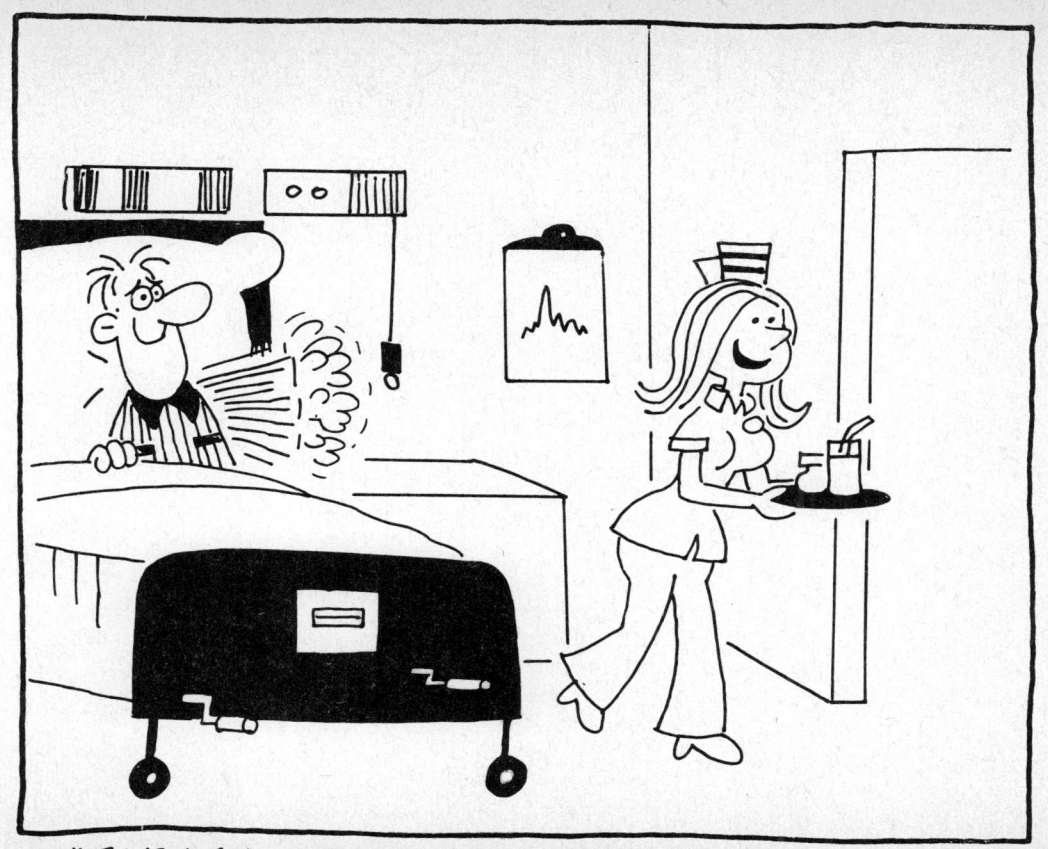

"IF YOU SHOULD WANT ME AGAIN, ALL YOU HAVE TO DO IS BUZZ THE BUZZER!"

"LET ME KNOW WHEN YOU'RE HIGH ENOUGH!"

PERHAPS, IN YOUR REAL LIFE, YOU ENJOYED DUCK A L'ORANGE WITH A FINE WINE. A TRIP TO A SUSHI BAR MAY HAVE SET YOUR GASTRIC JUICES TO FLOWING. MAINE LOBSTER AND DRAWN BUTTER, A CRISP SALAD WITH A LIGHT GARLIC DRESSING, HOME MADE FRENCH FRIES AND A COOL FROSTY ALE WOULD PERK UP THE OLD TASTE BUDS.

"I'M AFRAID THERE'S A LOT MORE WRONG WITH MRS. THOMAS THAN MEETS THE EYE --- SHE ACTUALLY ENJOYS HOSPITAL FOOD!"

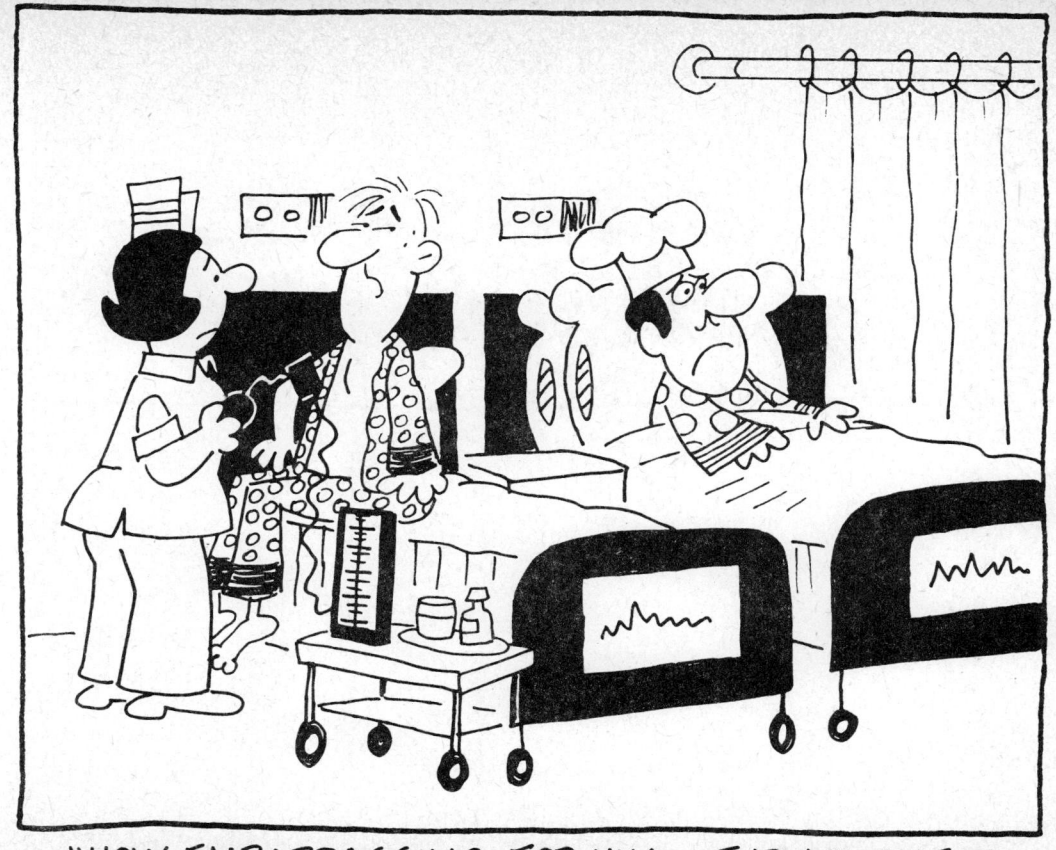
"HOW EMBARRASSING FOR HIM -- TURNED OUT IT WAS HIS OWN COOKING!"

"JUST A LITTLE WIDER PLEASE!"

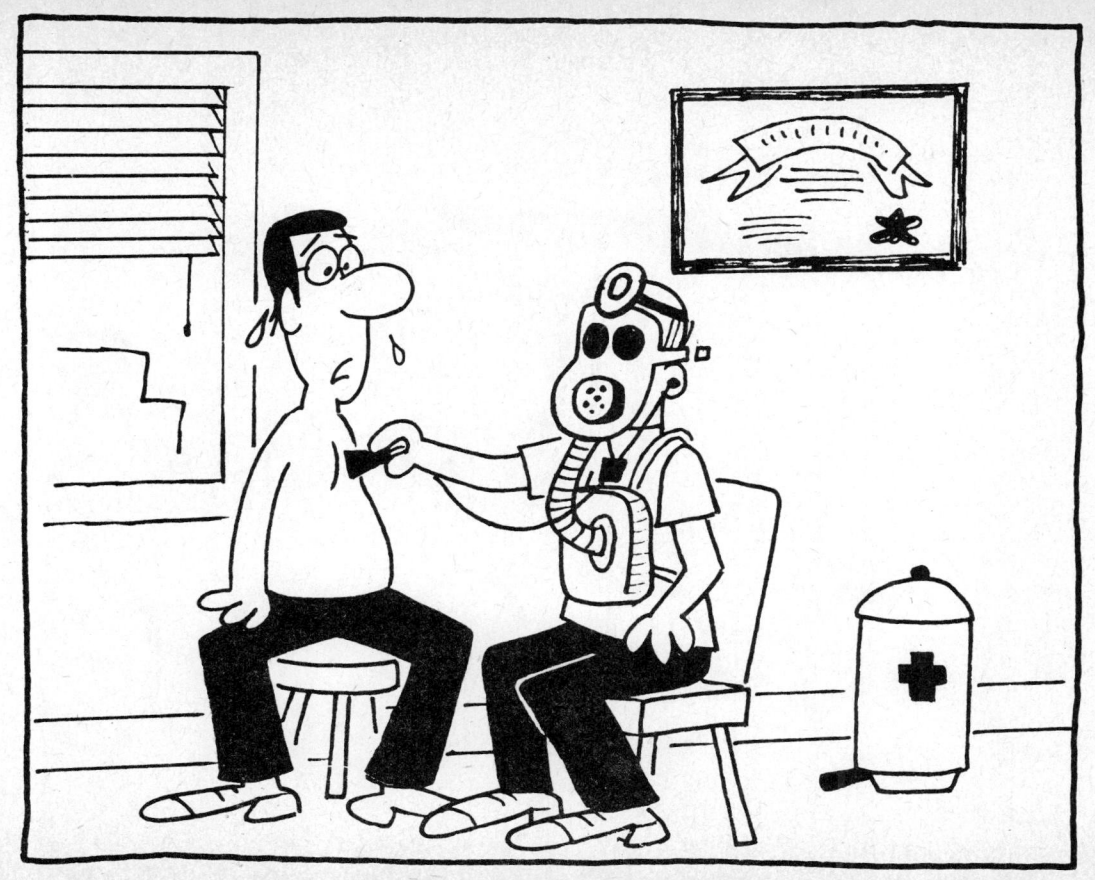

"TRY CHEWING YOUR FOOD MORE THOROUGHLY!"

"THIS PICTURE IS TAKING LONGER TO SHOOT THAN 'WAR AND PEACE'!!"

"CAN YOU LOOK INSIDE?—ONE OF OUR SPOONS IS MISSING!"

"JUST AS I SUSPECTED. YOU HAVE TENNIS ELBOW!"

"CONGRATULATIONS, MR. CRABTREE -- YOUR ACNE HAS FINALLY CLEARED UP!"

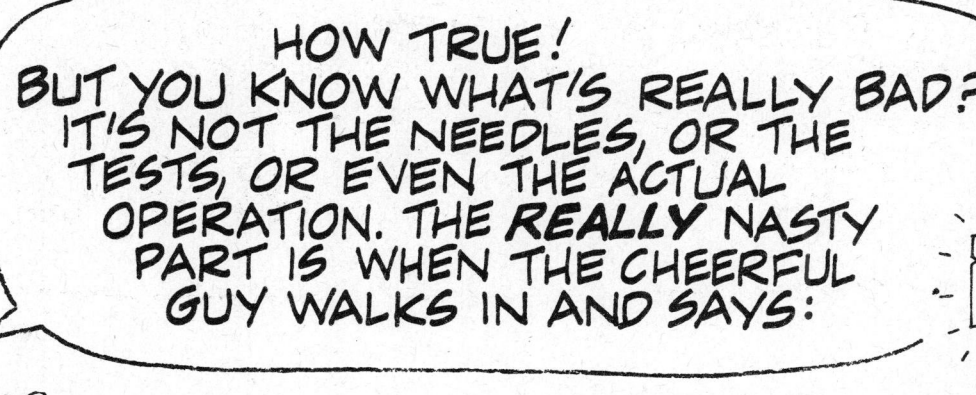

"HE'S A GOOD SURGEON, BUT HIS FIRST LOVE IS PEDIATRICS!"

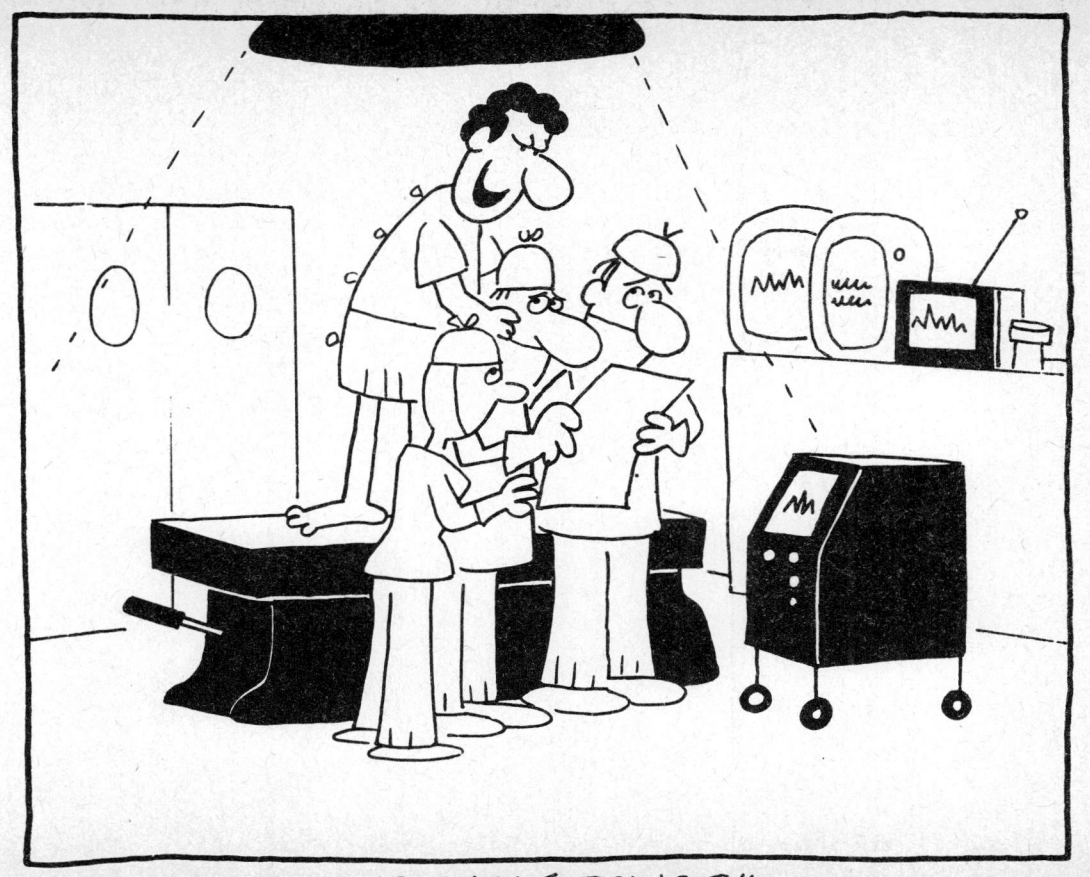

"THAT WIFE OF MINE JUST BOUGHT A NEW WARDROBE---MORE PENTOTHAL--FOR THAT ROUND-THE-WORLD-CRUISE WE'RE TAKING!"

It's over. At last.
And you know what they allllllllwayyyys say.
"There...there. Everythings going to
be aaaaaalllright.

It will be, too.

Ohhhh sure. You'll have some discomfort, and yes, it will take some time to get back to that old self. But, you'll do it.

And your family and friends will be such a big help........

"THERE'S NOTHING TO WORRY ABOUT. THE INSURANCE CAME THROUGH WITH FLYING COLORS!"

"LET ME KNOW WHEN VISITING HOURS ARE OVER!"

A few last important words with the doctor, and we'll be on our way.

YOU DON'T JUST WALK OUT AND TAKE YOUR LEAVE. REGULATIONS, MY FRIEND, REGULATIONS. THE NURSE MUST WHEEL YOU OUT, AND OFFICIALLY HAND YOU OVER TO YOUR TRANSPORTATION.

✱ PLEASE TURN TO PAGE 13

My stay in _____ hospital

began on _____ .

My Doctor _____ set me free on

_____ .

Comments: _____

_____

_____

_____

_____

_____